WESTCOUNTRY SAIL

Merchant Shipping 1840 - 1960

Brig entering Boscastle c 1850

The topsail schooner *Susan Vittery*, 140 tons, was built in 1859 by Kelly at Sandquay, Dartmouth for Vittery & Co of Brixham. She spent her first years in the Azores orange trade, later going into the Newfoundland codfish trade. From 1885 onwards she was owned by H. A. Hawkey of Newquay. A third mast was added in 1903. At the end of World War I she was practically rebuilt at Whitstable, and in 1923 was bought by Captain John Creenan of Ballinacurra, Co Cork and renamed *Brooklands*. She sailed until 1946 without an engine, but in 1953, sailing under her original name of *Susan Vittery*, she was lost near the Tuskar. This view of her is by A. de Clerk who painted ship portraits in Antwerp from 1870 to 1910.

WESTCOUNTRY SAIL

Merchant Shipping 1840 - 1960

Michael Bouquet

David & Charles : Newton Abbot

FOR JOYCE
WITH LOVE

ISBN 0 7153 5033 1

Set in 11 on 13 point Baskerville
and printed in Great Britain
by W J Holman Limited Dawlish
for David & Charles (Publishers) Limited
South Devon House Newton Abbot Devon

Contents

Introduction

Old photographs evoke strange memories; one sees a picture of a place one thinks one knows, but it is a delicately different place. Old photographs are piquant, nostalgic but above all mysterious, for they show landscapes which for all their familiarity are as strange as a lunar view or an ancient myth.

The broad view of the Westcountry maritime seascape is familiar enough, though it has changed rapidly in the last decade and is likely to change even more quickly in the future. In bringing together the pictures in this book, I have tried to recapture something of an entirely vanished scene—a maritime peep-show into a recent past.

It is a truism to equate the Westcountry with a seafaring tradition; 'sea-dogs of Devon' and 'Drake he was a Devon man' are familiar enough phrases. But it is historically justifiable to claim the nineteenth century as a golden age of Westcountry shipowning and seafaring, and to include within the term 'Westcountry' not only Devon, but Dorset, Somerset and Cornwall as well. The pictures in this book attempt t cover the Westcountry shipping scene from about 1840 to 1960. The purpose of this introduction is briefly to recapitulate the story of Westcountry ships and seamen before the beginning of the nineteenth century.

The first craft to sail our western waters are so far away in time as to be like vessels seen in a misty dream. The dugout canoes of the lake villagers of the Somerset marshes, the ships of

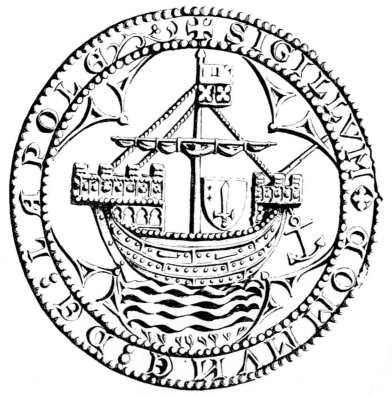

Fig 1
Single-masted ship on the
Common Seal of Poole
13th century

Fig 2
Chaucer's shipman goes
aboard the *Magdalene*

the Gaulish and Roman merchants which visited the Exe and Plym, the rude coracles of the Celtic saints who floated across the Severn Sea 'on hurdles', the Saxon ships which brought settlers up every creek and estuary, the Viking longships which raided Wessex in the ninth century; all these are insubstantial and tenuous. We know neither their names nor the names of their mariners. We can only deduce their build, their rig and the cargoes which they carried. Not until we come to the thirteenth century do we get representations of ships on the seals of Westcountry seaport towns—ships which are seaworthy and credible. Not until the beginning of the fourteenth century do we get the first named ships.

The corporation seal of Lyme Regis (1284) shows a single-masted ship of Viking type with a beast head on her high stem and stern posts. Her hull is of a double-ended clinker-built type with planking in short lengths. A step forward is to be seen in the thirteenth century seal of Poole (fig 1). Here is an example of how the temporary fighting stages fore and aft have become permanent structures, increased in length and secured to stem and stern posts, a step towards being built into the hull permanently as forecastle and poop.

These ships from the seals, in spite of being too short and too high, so as to be fitted within the circumference of the matrix, are the earliest representations of Westcountry ships. From the seals it is perfectly possible to deduce credible and seaworthy reconstructions.

These merchantmen carried the petty coastwise traffic, the wine from France and Spain, the pilgrims for Bordeaux en route for Santiago de Compostella, the tin, the hides and the wool. They are the ships in which merchants traded with the English provinces in France. They are the ships which assembled in the Dart for the second and third crusades; the ships

Fig 3 Typical mid-sixteenth-century shipping

of the fleet which the Black Prince gathered at Plymouth in 1355. They are real ships with named mariners and with identifiable names, such as the *Santi Salvatoris* of Plymouth of 1303 or the cog *Seinte Marie* of Exmouth of 1310. The latter was hired by her owners to the Exeter municipal authorities for the king's service in the Irish Sea. The records of this transaction give not only the names of the *Seinte Marie's* five owners, but those of her twenty-eight mariners—sailors with the names Wauter de Ilfridecumbe, Cosyn Edward, Richard Gille and Richard atte mershe de Pouderham. This document drawn up between the owners and the city authorities shows not only the difficulties of forming a royal fleet out of individual ships, but also the wiles practised by owners and mariners to earn a dishonest penny from the royal exchequer.

The margin between honesty and dishonesty, between peace and war was fluid. Given the contemporary context this is understandable. When Bishop Grandisson came to Exeter in the fourteenth century he wrote of himself as having come *in culo mundi*—to the edge of the world. To the medieval mind the south-western peninsula of England jutting into the Western Ocean was indeed an ultimate extremity. The sea was here with a swiftly moving range of tides; the sparsely inhabited coasts, iron-bound yet indented with creeks and estuaries, were the home of much petty commerce. The single-masted ships were small and unweatherly. Profits were so hardly won that the temptation to take short cuts was almost irresistible to the thrusting and resourceful seamen of the west.

Chaucer's shipman, a character possibly based upon John Hawley of Dartmouth (died 1408), was one of these men. In his *Magdalene* he knew the coasts from Scotland to Finisterre and down across the Bay of Biscay. A drunken sea-bear who had few qualms about broaching cargo or practising piracy, he knew his Channel ports, his tides, his currents and his simple navigation. His weatherbeaten figure lurches into the *Canterbury Tales,* riding like a sack and breathing vinous good fellowship, the protagonist of many a Westcountry mariner in the centuries to follow (fig 2).

By the fifteenth century the ships of the western ports were growing larger and were sailing farther afield. That notorious pirate Harry Paye of Poole was pillaging ships on the Biscayan coast of Spain. A Saltash ship, the *Nicholas,* sailed for Finmark within the Arctic Circle, and a Fowey ship was trading to Iceland at a time when Fowey was infamous as a pirates' haunt, terrorising the western approaches to the Channel. By the beginning of the fifteenth century the two-masted ship was appearing in Mediterranean waters, and by the second half of the century the three-master had appeared in northern Europe, so that by 1500 it was a normal rig in the narrow seas.

A picture map of Plymouth made for Henry VIII in 1539 shows not only the sea defences of the port, but the whole panorama of early Tudor shipping. There are the oared ferry-boats at Cremyll and Saltash, and the single-masted barges crowd the quays in Sutton harbour and Stonehouse. But a three-master is bound up the Hamoaze, another is at anchor in the Cattewater and a third is entering the Sound under sail. Under the lee of Drake's Island there is even a great four-master, one of the most modern ships of the day (fig 3).

The three-masted sailing ship square-rigged on two masts with a lateen on the mizzen and a high-steeved bowsprit was the ship in which Westcountrymen of the sixteenth century sailed for far-off seas (fig 4). Dartmouth pioneered the Newfoundland trade and Poole was not far behind. William Hawkins sent his ship *Paule* from Plymouth to Brazil three times between 1530 and 1532. His son John was on the Guinea coast buying slaves by 1562. Early in the century Westcountry seamen were lready organising and executing successful privateering ventures. As early as 1549 Walter Raleigh of East Budleigh—father of the great Sir Walter—organised the capture of a rich Spanish merchantman attempting to enter Dartmouth.

These were the years of the three-master; the years of Drake's circumnavigation, of the Spanish wars, of the rapid growth in the number of ships putting out from the South West to Newfoundland and the American colonies. The three-masted rig became more complex, so that there are considerable differences between a three-master of say 1550, and one of 1700. During the same period the two-master had increased in size and importance, so that the brig

Fig 4 Typical three-master c 1600

9

Fig 5 Late eighteenth-century brig and fullrigger

and the snow became the typical sailing ships of the middle and latter eighteenth century. The Torquay ship *Buckland,* William Bartlett of St Marychurch master, whose adventures on a passage from St John's, Newfoundland to Torbay in November 1755 are the subject of a crudely spirited primitive painting in the Torquay Museum, was a three-master. The *Albion,* built at Bideford in 1785, whose account book and likeness on an engraved glass goblet are preserved at Bideford, was a two-master—a brig (figs 5 and 6).

These then were the merchant ships of south-west England in the early nineteenth century. They were three-masted square-riggers, either ships or barques, usually well under 300 tons, old-fashioned in hull-form and rig. There was a whole range of two-masters, from brigs or snows as large as some of the three-masters, down to the tiny pole-masted brigs of North Devon, some less than 50 tons. There was a growing fleet of weatherly topsail schooners, many in the Azores or the Mediterranean trades. There were scores of single-masted smacks and sloops, some of them ocean-going craft sailing to the Azores, but most were barges in the estuaries of the Fal and Tamar.

All these rigs were depicted by contemporary artists: in heavy oils with sails of stiff board-like canvas and regular white-topped waves; in crisp water colour or gouache—'The *Try Again* entering the Port of Leghorn'; or in black and white line engraving in which the scale is cleverly manipulated to exaggerate the size of the ship.

Just before 1850 the camera made its appearance in the Westcountry. At least one photographer was taking pictures of ships at Plymouth in 1849 and by 1855 the ship was already a favoured subject for the new race of photographic artists (see pages 26, 48 and 58). The old marine artists continued their work for many years, particularly in North Sea ports, on the Continent and in Mediterranean ports. The last of these, Reuben Chappell, who lived at Par, went on painting ship portraits up to the 1930s.

10

By the end of the century commercial photographers such as York of Bristol were finding it profitable to concentrate on shipping. Increasingly there was a demand first for photographic views and later for picture postcards for sale to visitors. As photography became technically easier, the amateur found that ships and harbours made splendid subjects for his camera. Very largely as a result of F. G. G. Carr's lecture on *Surviving Types of coastal craft in the British Isles* given to the Society for Nautical Research in 1934, serious interest was aroused in small ships and small ports. Because for various reasons small merchant ships and small maritime communities survived there for longer than elsewhere in the British Isles, south-west England has been particularly rich in illustrative material. Basil Greenhill has made studies in the history of sea transport in the South West for a particular period, in a detail which is now probably impossible to match elsewhere.

This book is my own personal choice of favourite pictures from the artist and the photographer to illustrate the theme of merchant sail in the South West of England. Such is the variety of material available from so many sources that I could have filled these pages twice over. Of necessity there are omissions; to those who cannot find their favourite port or their favourite vessel I can only put forward these pictures as an attempt to show the small ports of the South West as they were when they held—as the old men still remember—'a forest of masts'.

Fig 6 Brig of about 1800

Every Westcountry port could match the scene in this photograph. Taken on a Sunday afternoon in 1913, it shows the schooner *Hannah Ransom* warping out between the piers at Bridport (West Bay). The onlookers in their Sunday best are no more in numbers than the normal crowd which came down to see a vessel entering or leaving the harbour. The *Hannah Ransom* belonged to George Alford of Bridport, coal and gravel merchant, from 1892 to 1913. She brought the best Wallsend coal, sold at 1s 6d a hundredweight early in the century. She carried away gravel and sand for Scotland, Hull or London. As she warps out, jibs and topsails have been loosed and foresail set; the big mainsail is still not completely hoisted. At that time sailing vessels were hauled out to a buoy 280yd from the entrance. This picture is entirely typical of the Westcountry when similar arrivals and departures from little ports were occurring daily. The crowd assembled to watch the sailing of this very ordinary schooner reflects something of the interest and indeed affection which small communities felt for the ships which served them.

The *Hannah Ransom*, 104 tons, was built at Crosshouse near Southampton in 1870. She went ashore at Sizewell Gap, Aldeburgh in November 1919 and became a total loss.

Round the Coast

In the next forty pages we make a cruise into the ports of the South West in the high noon and in the golden afternoon of the sailing ship era. We do not enter the naval anchorages at Portland or the Hamoaze; nor do we visit what were primarily fishing harbours. Our concern is with merchant shipping. Many of the vessels illustrated were not Westcountry ships at all; that they came from the Baltic, from the Low Countries, from the Mediterranean or even from North America, was a measure of the West's importance in nineteenth-century maritime commerce.

As one enters Dorset from the east one has the feeling of entering Wessex; as one sails down-Channel, Poole is surely the first of the Westcountry ports. Here Meadus built the *Waterwitch* in 1871 (page 63). Up to the 1920s sailing ships called here to discharge timber and to load clay. In this photograph taken at the turn of the century there are visible a brig, topsail schooners and ketches. The *Hematope* of Bideford in the foreground was built at Paspebiac, Canada in 1845 and was originally rigged as a brigantine. By the end of the century she was owned in Appledore, and in true Appledore style she was re-rigged as a ketch. Her successive Appledore owners were William Hutchings of the Bell Inn, and George Eastlake who was also her master. After nearly seventy years afloat the *Hematope* went ashore on the rocks at West Appledore and was condemned.

In the 1920s beautiful Italian sailing ships came to Poole to load china clay for Savona in northern Italy. Two of these photographs were taken aboard the wooden brigantine *Avvenire* of Viareggio. She was built at Chiavari in 1906.

Below, the barquentine *Patria* of Viareggio makes sail as she leaves Poole. A wooden vessel of 461 tons, she was built at Oneglia in 1920.

Unlike Poole, Swanage is not an ancient borough. In the nineteenth century it was a village growing into a resort. Its maritime trade was in locally quarried Purbeck stone, but the coming of the railway from Wareham in 1887 killed the port. In the photograph above taken in the 1890s an excursion steamer and a schooner provide the sole evidence of maritime activity.

Weymouth was a medieval port which became a resort in the eighteenth century, but sailing ships frequented it until World War I. Schooners were built and owned here. A Weymouth schooner, the *Lizzie,* is shown on page 38.

Bridport—or West Bay—is an ancient port which even today attracts a few coasters. Once it was famed for wooden shipbuilding of high quality (pages 60 and 76). The picture below, taken at the turn of the century, shows country people in their Sunday best, come to look at the schooners on the quay—a typical scene in any small provincial seaport.

Modern seaborne trade passes Lyme by, but once it was a busy port serving a wide hinter-land (page 57). Once, deepwater ships were launched here like the barque *Lyme Regis* of 250 tons, built by Mansfield in 1849. She was probably the largest ship ever constructed in Lyme, but she was only one of a number of vessels. Her builder's son, J. B. Mansfield, started up in business at Teignmouth soon after the *Lym Regis* was launched, and by 1853 he had a hundred men working for him. Early in the nineteenth century Lyme shipyards, with those of Bridport and Topsham, were noted for fast-sailing smacks for the London to Leith packet trade. Even at the end of the century the ancient Cobb was still crowded with small coasters.

Long ago the Axe estuary was a fine natural harbour; at Sidmouth and Budleigh Salterton colliers once discharged on the open beach. But the Exe estuary is our next real port of call. The fishing villages of Exmouth and Topsham had become important shipping centres by the nineteenth century. The shipyards of Redway at Exmouth and Holman at Topsham (page 78) built many deepwater traders. The Exeter Canal claims to be the oldest lock canal in England. Its upper portion dates from 1566 but it was enlarged in 1676 and extended to Turf in 1825-31. It is navigable by ships 131ft long, with a beam of 26ft and drawing 14ft of water —dimensions which have inhibited the growth of Exeter as a modern port.

At the end of the last century the Norwegian barque *Statsraad Broch* was lying at Bull Hill in the Exe estuary taking in ballast; one can see the tackles rigged from the main yard. Also visible is the windmill pump so typical of the wooden timber-carrying ships. The windmill kept working as long as there was any breeze, and its interminable 'onk . . . ur . . . onk . . . ur' as it pumped away gave the timber ships the name of 'onkers'. The *Statsraad Broch* was a wooden barque of 322 tons, built at Svelvik in 1869 and owned in Christiania.

Sailing vessels using the canal were towed up to Exeter from Turf by horse, no doubt to the annoyance of the numerous anglers along the towpath. Horse towage cost $2\frac{1}{2}$d a ton in 1865.

The coming of auxiliary power to sailing coasters in the 1920s (page 69) eased the passage of the canal. Here the steel ketch *Mary Eliezer,* 58 tons, built at Hammelwarden, Germany in 1904, motors up the canal. Despite her Hull registration she is one of the Braunton fleet of ketches. Her topmast is housed and her bowsprit steeved-up all ready for her discharge in Exeter Basin.

Two topsail schooners wait for the tide at Turf. The vessel on the left is strictly a standing topgallant schooner, that on the right a double topsail schooner. The dimensions of Turf locks governed the size of ships using the canal. When the Dutch schooner *Trio* of Groningen arrived there in 1938 with 375 tons of basic slag for Exeter, her bowsprit had to be sawn off to allow her to enter Turf lock.

Costly improvements were made to the canal from 1825 to 1831. An artificial basin 900ft in length was excavated at the head of the canal and access to Exeter Quay was given by the King's Arms sluice. The quay and its massive warehouses dating from 1835 were still used by sailing vessels well into the present century. Here a big standing topgallant-yard schooner is discharging cargo and drying her sails, while the masts and sails of other vessels can be seen in the distance.

Even after the railway came to Exeter, sailing vessels with bulk cargoes of coal, timber and cement came up to the quay. In this photograph the topsail schooner *Abeja* of Exeter, 174 tons, built at Littlehampton in 1881, lies by the ballast heaps in front of Colleton Buildings.

The City Basin was opened on Michaelmas Day 1830 when the *Ranger* was the first ship to enter. This faded photograph of the basin taken at the turn of the century shows the crowded effect given by the masts and spars of only half a dozen small sailing ships.

Something of this effect is being re-created at the International Sailing Craft Association's Exeter Maritime Museum opened in 1969. With some of the craft moored in the basin and others displayed in the imposing warehouses, the museum is already bringing to life again what had become a run-down area of the city. When the *Nonsuch* ketch, the replica of a seventeenth-century trader built at Appledore for the Hudson Bay Company in 1968, berthed at the basin in August 1969, something of the old atmosphere of life and bustle reappeared.

20

Teignmouth has only been a port of registry since 1853, but ships have crossed its bar since the Middle Ages. From 1800 it has been associated with the shipment of ball clay which is exported to all parts of Europe. At one time the clay was brought down the Teign in barges and transhipped to vessels lying in the stream. Here between the wars is the auxiliary Finnish schooner *Saturn* of Mariehamn with clay barges alongside. She was built at Werki, Finland in 1913; her home port of Mariehamn in the Aaland Islands was famous as the home of the last fleet of ocean-going sail in Europe. The pinched-in elliptical stern, the neatly turned railing round the poop, the big deckhouse and the very lofty topmasts are all typical of wooden schooners from the Gulf of Finland. The *Saturn* has no topsail yards but she carries a foreyard from which to set a squaresail when running before the wind.

We think of Torquay as a leading holiday resort, but in the nineteenth century it was a busy little seaport sending emigrants to Canada (page 58) and even building ships. Here is a typical scene in Torquay harbour in the 1850s. The snow *Sarah Fleming* built at North Shields in 1833, and the brigantine *Dynamene* built at Lyme as a smack in 1818 and rebuilt at Paignton in 1855, lie alongside the quay. Both ships belonged to John Crossman, a local timber merchant, and traded to North America. The *Sarah Fleming* regularly took parties of emigrants to Quebec en route for the mid-West.

Behind the ships and outside the harbour are the slipway and yard of William Shaw the shipbuilder (page 79). In the foreground are the coal sheds where the colliers discharged.

The tower of St John's is still incomplete, so we can date this picture to about 1882. Torquay had established itself as a holiday resort, but in the foreground a little topgallant-yard schooner is seen unloading timber—note the charming hand crane; across the harbour a brigantine has almost finished unloading coal on Vaughan Parade. Meanwhile the cabmen wait for the visitors.

Brixham had over fifty shipbuilders operating at various times in the nineteenth century. The favourite rig among the vessels built in the town was the topsail schooner. Here is one of the many Brixham-built schooners, the *Via,* launched by Upham in 1864 for the Newfoundland trade. She survived until 1931.

We scarcely think of Paignton as a haven for merchant shipping, but the little harbour built in 1839 once had a steady business of coasting trade. Here in the 1870s, long before the visitors came, a tiny schooner has put in to unload timber.

Dartmouth has been important as a sheltered deepwater port since the twelfth century. A hundred years ago it was still significant as a building port for fast weatherly schooners for the Azores fruit trade. Of these the *Susan Vittery* was the last to survive (frontispiece). Dartmouth had a long connection with the Newfoundland trade. One of Newman's brigantines, the *Harrier* (164 tons, built at Northam near Southampton in 1856), is being towed out of the harbour on a Newfoundland voyage about 1870, beneath the guns of the castle. She has her fore-and-afters set, but none of her squaresails.

Salcombe and Kingsbridge had at least eight nineteenth-century shipbuilders who between them launched nearly 250 vessels. A typical example was the *Speedy*, 116 tons, a St Michaels fruit schooner built by Date at Dodbrook in 1852. During the orange season, November to April, these small vessels had to force their way to the westward in ballast and return with a highly perishable cargo in the worst weather of the year. Like many a schooner built for the Azores trade, the *Speedy* later entered the Newfoundland fish trade (pages 59 and 66).

This vintage photograph was taken about 1853 from Cremyll, on the present site of Mashford's yard. It looks across to Mutton Cove with Richmond Walk and Devonport and the Monument behind. In the centre is a perfect little brig; she could be any one of the 538 merchantmen which entered Plymouth from foreign ports in a typical year in mid-century. She is a beauty. Single topsail yards are squared to perfection, topsails clewed up to the quarters of the yards, 'pig's ears' hanging in the bunt, all the marks of a real old-timer.

The upper tidal reaches of the Tamar are among the most fascinating of the inland waterways of England. Here are the ruins of a deserted industrial landscape. Here in the nineteenth century came small sailing ships to bring coal and timber for the mines and to carry away copper, tin and arsenic. Only a short way from the head of navigation, vessels like this schooner (opposite above) came to load copper ore from the Mary Tavy mines. Carried along the 4 miles of the Tavistock canal, the copper was transferred to trolleys running down the inclined plane in the background, through the tunnel under the cottages and the field in the middle distance, and thence to the quays. This deserted river port of Morwellham is to be brought to life again under imaginative plans proposed by the Dartington Hall Trust.

On 23 May 1907 they were still building the Calstock viaduct. Under the shadow of the sixth arch on the Devon side James Goss was building his ketch *Garlandstone*, begun in 1905 as the foundations were being dug for the piers of the viaduct. The *Garlandstone* was completed in 1909 and still survives. The big schooner in the foreground is discharging coal for mines on the Cornish side of the river.

On 22 August 1915 the three-masted schooner *James W. Fisher* of Barrow appeared off Looe under full sail, just too late on tide to enter the port. She had been built at Kingston, Co Elgin back in 1874 for Fishers of Barrow, a firm still busy in coastal and short-sea trades.

The following afternoon at high water the *James W. Fisher* came into port and alongside the quay, watched by a thin crowd on that wartime summer day. Alas, within a year she was lost on the Anglesey coast.

Fowey is the queen of Cornish havens, a wonderful sheltered deepwater anchorage. Since the schooner *Rippling Wave* loaded the first cargo of china clay to leave the port in April 1869, Fowey has been associated with this export. In the nineteenth century its ships were foremost in the Newfoundland trade. A few sailing ships are waiting at the buoys early in this century to go up to the clay tips. Left is the steel barque *Colbert* of Genoa, 810 tons, built at Bordeaux in 1872. Astern of the *Colbert* are two delightful little Danes ready to go under the clay tips. They have actually unbolted their galleys from the deck and shifted them to one side to be clear of the shutes. On the schooner nearest the camera the galley is visible jammed in between the foremast and the rigging.

Hidden from the town of Fowey and from the anchorage are the clay tips from where ships carry china clay all over the world. Here on 21 September 1907 one could have seen these vessels—a big fore-and-aft schooner from the Baltic, a barque, and astern of them a delightful little brigantine probably Italian.

Such was the nineteenth-century importance of Fowey as a sailing ship port that one can find many other examples of Fowey-owned sailing ships in this book (see pages 59, 62, 63, 79 and 92).

Par harbour owes its origins to Joseph Thomas Austen (later Treffry), who in 1828-36 went ahead with his scheme for an artificial harbour linked to nearby copper and tin mines. The mines closed one by one, but their loss was more than replaced by the expanding china clay industry.

This picture, taken before 1914, recaptures the scene at Par when sometimes—as old men remember—it was possible for an active boy to walk, scramble and swing right across the harbour on the decks of sailing vessels. Here ships came from all over Britain and from northern Europe to load clay. Many came to Tregaskes' dry dock for repair and for survey. Here Reuben Chappell (page 102) recorded them in watercolour. In the foreground is a Yorkshire schooner, the *John Martin* of Goole, built at Knottingley in 1865.

Charlestown is almost the smallest of the Cornish harbours. Because of its tiny size a few ships seem to fill it up, and these three photographs give a splendid impression of its crowded quays, the masts and yards of little vessels, the pervading white dust of the clay, the broad-wheeled clay waggons of a local design peculiar to the clay trade and the great horses which hauled them. This picture, taken some time in the 1880s, shows on the left the schooner *Crystal Palace* of Dublin, built at Arklow in 1855.

In the second picture (right) taken before 1900 there are five schooners and a brigantine all loading clay, except for one which is discharging coal. Again the clay waggons are much in evidence. In the days before motor transport these waggons, suitably spruced-up, were much in demand for Sunday School outings and for trips to local beaches. This picture is full of detail: for example in the nearest schooner the hatch-covers fore side of the main hatch, the sentry-box lavatory in the fore rigging and the tiller steering.

In the third picture, taken from the seaward end of the harbour in the 1920s, we have a French ketch and two Dutch schooners. On the right is one of these, the *Zeehond* of Terneuzen, a steel vessel built in Groningen in 1914. She once sailed from Newfoundland to Gibraltar in 17 days.

Mevagissey, once the subject of a coarse remark among coasting seamen, reflecting on its alleged lack of sanitary facilities, was really a fishing port, though it was certainly visited by a number of small coasters. Here is one of them, the *Snowflake* of Runcorn, drying her sails after discharging coal. Built by Brundritt of Runcorn in 1880 for the Newfoundland trade in which she continued to sail almost up to the Great War, she has the typical Irish Sea stern with 'the rudder out-of-doors'. She was later owned by M. Thomas of Plymouth and in the 1920s and 1930s by her master Captain J. Pinch. In 1935 she was sold to an Austrian buyer and left Par for the Adriatic. She survived the war and was still listed in *Lloyd's Register* in the late 1950s as the Yugoslav *Hvrat*.

'Falmouth for orders' was the destination of many a sailing ship from 1848, when Britain was thrown open to the importation of foreign wheat, until 1939. Most of the world's big sailing ships anchored there at some time for a few days while the final destination of their grain cargo was decided. When this photograph was taken in July 1922 St Anthony's Point lighthouse still had its fogwarning bell—the heaviest bell in Cornwall. This was removed in 1954 and has since been melted down. The four-masted barque at anchor is the German *Magdalene Vinnen*, 3,476 tons, built at Kiel in 1921. She had an auxiliary engine but used her canvas to a considerable degree. She sails today as the Russian *Sedov*.

Milton's 'great Vision of the guarded mount' looks out across Mounts Bay as three Cornish schooners try their paces against each other some time back in the 1880s. How nostalgic this old picture is. It conjures up the days of what the old sailors called 'wooden ships and iron men', of tar and hemp, of ships at one with the rugged Mount and the bleak Cornish landscape.

Penzance has a capacious harbour overlooked by the nineteenth-century gothic of St Mary's church. The topsail schooner *Mary Barrow* of Barrow is beside the quay. Built by W. H. Lean at Falmouth in 1891 as a standing topgallant-yard schooner for trade to the Rio Grande, she was a magnificent specimen of a trading schooner. By 1928, when this photograph was taken, she had only two yards on the fore. Soon afterwards she was re-registered at Truro under the ownership of Captain M. P. Mortensen, 'Peter the Dane'. She was fitted with an engine and her rig further reduced (see page 69). She was lost on the Calf of Man in the week of the Munich crisis in 1938.

Newlyn was noted for its fishing fleet but it was visited too by sailing coasters (see page 66). On 14 October 1910 the schooner *Lizzie* of Weymouth was at anchor off Newlyn in shoal water in a strong SSE wind, and labouring heavily. The *Elizabeth and Blanche* pulling lifeboat stood by her, while she slipped her anchors and ran for the harbour. The *Lizzie* was built by E. Ellis at Nevin in 1850 as the brigantine *Catherine & Alice*, 98 tons.

Round the Land—the ketch *Result* of Barnstaple (page 102ff) passes inside the Longships under sail and power through an intricate and seldom used passage between the Kettle's Bottom and the Peal.

Smeaton's pier (1766-70) shelters the harbour of St Ives. Many sailing ships were owned here and one major shipowning firm, the Hain Steamship Co, had its origin in small family-owned schooners sailing out of the port. The bottom of the harbour is of sand coated with shingle. In this picture, taken early in this century, some schooners lie aground, moored head and stern. The centre vessel, the *Atlas* of Wexford, has unshackled her cable from the anchor and made it fast to a mooring rope. The schooner on the right with her overhanging stern has all the looks of an old Brixham or Dartmouth-built fruit carrier of the type of the *Susan Vittery*.

Schooners were built and owned in the bar harbour of Hayle, and in the tiny havens of Portreath and St Agnes (page 81), but the next port of any size along this coast is Newquay where there were once four shipyards and nearly 200 vessels owned in the port. Here the usual crowd is at the pierheads to see the locally owned schooner *Cavalier* leave harbour.

At Padstow there were five shipyards. This picture, taken on Regatta Day 1913, shows an interesting variety of now completely obsolete types of both sail and steam.

At one time vessels came ashore on the open beach beneath the castle at Tintagel to discharge cargoes. This smack photographed in the mid-seventies is possibly the *Bee*.

Timber was once imported direct from Quebec to the tiny harbour of Boscastle (see vignette on page 1), where a small tiller-steered ketch is seen unloading coal in baskets, using a hand winch and the ship's own gear.

Bude was a problem port, hard to enter and often harder still to leave. Boatmen known as 'hobblers' came out of Bude, as at many other ports, to assist vessels by taking their ropes and making them fast to the buoys or booms which marked the channel, so that the crew could warp the vessel to the lock gates. Not only were many small ships owned in Bude; some, like the *Annie Davey*, were built there. She was launched in 1872 by one of the Stapleton family who constructed several vessels in Bude between 1835 and 1878, launching them sideways into the canal. Owned by Oliver Davey of Bude, the *Annie Davey* was run down on the East Coast in 1908.

From Bude, north to Hartland the coast runs steep-to and ironbound, open to the force of the Atlantic. Once there was a tiny haven at Hartland Quay, destroyed by gales at the end of the last century. Traders such as the smack *Susanna* came here to discharge cargoes behind the shelter of the curving stone pier,

> Where upon Hartland's tempest furrowed shore
> Breaks the long swell from farthest Labrador.

From Clovelly the smack *Ebenezer* (the outside vessel), built at Bideford in 1845, used to sail to Newport to load 28 tons of coals for Squire Heaven of Lundy, discharging on the island's landing beach. James Braund (page 83) was her skipper. Besides running to Lundy she took cargoes to Bideford, Bucksh and Clovelly, and even to Hartland and Boscastle.

Some of the last sail-using vessels in the British Isles set out from over the Bar of Taw and Torridge. Here, as shown in this photograph taken early in the century, Braunton or Appledore vessels sail down the channel to cross the Bar. In the background is the lighthouse on Braunton Burrows; in the foreground the track of the Bideford to Westward Ho! railway, open from 1901 to 1917. The channel out to the Bar is 2 sea miles long and in places only 100 yards wide; and its passage needed knowledge and skill.

Appledore itself was a village of ships, boats, sailors and shipyard workers. In 1921 the Northam Urban District, which includes Appledore, had 108 men per thousand engaged in seafaring occupations; the next highest proportion in the county was Dartmouth with 65 per thousand. For Devon as a whole the proportion was 10 per thousand. This photograph was taken about 1890. A brigantine is alongside the quay with a schooner and ketches moored outside. A topsail schooner and gravel barges are outward bound under sail.

'A forest of masts' is the phrase the old men commonly used to describe Appledore quay in the days of sail. This picture of windships and windrows taken before 1900 emphasises the essentially rural background to Appledore shipowning.

Higher up the Torridge at East-the-Water opposite Bideford the topgallant-yard schooner *Ebenezer* of Padstow is seen discharging building materials at the turn of the century. Under her stern a gravel barge is having some repairs done to her bottom. The *Ebenezer*, 88 tons, was built at Cardiff in 1869.

Four sailing ships at Castle Quay, Barnstaple in December 1927. Left to right: the Braunton ketch *Clara May*, 52 tons, built at Plymouth in 1891, the Danish topgallant-yard schooners *Hans* (1907) and *Niels* (1900), and the Danish barquentine *Fuglen* (1884). All these three were built and owned in Marstal and all had brought deals from the Baltic.

Up Braunton Pill came the little ketches with coal for the nearby villages. At 7 am on a May morning in 1930 the ketch *Ann*, built at Kingsbridge in 1889, approaches Vellator quay with coal from Lydney. One of her crew, John Marley of Lynmouth, has already come ashore with his kitbag. He's casting off the rope from the kedge, but he's in a hurry to catch the early train from Barnstaple to Lynton to get home to work aboard a Campbell steamer for the summer. In the boat is Jack Mitchell, mate of the other ketch, the *Bessie*, built at Milford in 1900. She belongs to Mr Incledon the coal merchant. Tom Slee is by the foremast of his own ketch, the *Ann* (see page 85). Both ketches have discharging gaffs rigged ready to begin unloading with their own gear. A tiny fragment of village history, but typical of Braunton shipowning.

This was the coast along which the Braunton and Appledore men sailed their little vessels. Here the Braunton-owned *Dido C,* so old that no one knew the date of her launch in Sweden, is precariously balanced on the rocks of Morte Point in September 1936. Strangely enough she came off safely and survived until 1947.

Another Braunton ketch, the tiny *Enid,* built at Pembroke Dock in 1898, cheats the tide under sail and motor at the western end of the Valley of Rocks near Lynmouth, just after passing Woody Bay. She has the pinched-in, cocked-up stern of the Milford Haven-built ships, vulgarly known in North Devon as 'guze arsed'.

Ilfracombe sheltering behind its ancient pier built by the Bourchiers, once lords of the manor, was a haven of refuge for small outward-bound ships in a sou-westerly gale—'Sir Bourchier's wind' as the local hobblers called it. A rare collection of ancient craft—two schooners and a brig—take the ground beneath St Nicholas' Chapel on Lantern Hill in the early 1850s.

Below, a crowded harbour at the end of the century. Left is the ketch *Trio*, built at Bideford in 1861; centre is the ketch *Cruiser*, built for Squire Bassett at Watermouth in 1867 (see page 50); right, the only ship built at Langport, Somerset to be listed in *Lloyd's Register*, the trow *Thorney* (1847). Her canvas side-cloths are typical of these undecked, open-hold vessels. Astern of these three are many ketches with a brigantine alongside the quay.

27 May 1905—the ketch *Emily* has come to Hele beach near Ilfracombe with the
year's supply of coal for Berrynarbor. Discharge is complete, and the gang of men
who have unloaded her, the farm cart with the last load, and a huddle of children
pause for the photographer. The *Emily* was built in Jersey in 1861, and when this
picture was taken she was owned by Captain Jack Irwin of Chambercombe. Later she
was owned in the Scilly Isles, where some of her timbers still survive—as fencing posts.

In the tiny cove at Watermouth, under the nineteenth-century gothic castle, lies the ketch *Olive & Mary* registered at Barnstaple. When this picture was taken in the first decade of this century the *Olive & Mary*, 37 tons and built at Rye in 1877, was owned by James Irwin senior of Combe Martin. She survived until 1927.

Less than 2 miles away at Combe Martin is a narrow beach protected by a weir of stones submerged at high water. Here came smacks with housecoal, like the *Sir T. D. Acland*, 40 tons, launched by the Stapletons at Bude in 1861. When this picture was taken about 1890 she was owned by George Irwin of Combe Martin.

Smacks and ketches came to Lynmouth with coal and groceries, beer and building materials and sailed away with bark for the tanneries (see page 68). This photograph was taken before the cliff railway was built in 1889 on the initiative of Sir George Newnes. Left is the ketch *Penguin*, owned by John Rea of Porlock, a few miles along the coast. A small fleet of schooners and ketches sailed out of the little haven of Porlock Weir. The *Penguin* was built at Port Glasgow in 1858 and has the typical round stern of the northern Irish Sea type, with the rudder 'out-of-doors' (see page 34).

Right is the ketch *Conservator* built at Padstow in 1843. She was owned by Philip Burgess of Lynmouth. The *Penguin* foundered in a November gale in 1901 bound from Appledore to Cardiff with gravel. The *Conservator* was lost after being in collision with the Italian barque *Concezione* while she was bound from Cardiff to Lynmouth with coal in January 1890.

This panoramic view of Minehead Quay taken about 1883 shows three local craft against the ancient seventeenth-century stone quay built by the Luttrells of Dunster Castle. All three vessels are owned by the Ridler family, who had interests in both farming and in the timber trade. Left is the *Argo,* launched at Swansea in 1868. She was built of Somerset timber shipped across in John Ridler's vessels from Lynmouth, Porlock and Minehead. In 1876 the *Argo* made a voyage to Gijon for nuts but she normally traded in the Bristol Channel. Originally a smack, she became a ketch in the early 1880s and was sold to Appledore owners in 1894.

Centre is the *John and William,* a smack launched at the back of the little dock at Porlock Weir. John Ridler owned her in partnership with her master, William Pulsford of Porlock. She was lost on Barry Beach in December 1894.

On the right is the pride of the Minehead fleet, the *Perriton,* named after the Ridlers' family home. Thomas Kent Ridler had her built on Minehead beach in 1881, employing a Watchet shipbuilder, Ben Williams. Williams had served his time in a Bridgwater shipyard, sailed to China and Australia in the full-rigger *Queen of England,* built some of the first craft on the Columbia River, and returned to Somerset to build the *Perriton.* She was the first ship launched at Minehead since Squire Luttrell had had the smack *Unanimity* built in 1798. The *Perriton* took eighteen months to build; a thousand spectators saw her launched; she survived until 1918 when she was sunk by a German submarine.

Watchet, whence Coleridge's Ancient Mariner reputedly sailed, has been a port since improvements were made in the early eighteenth century to an ancient stone quay. Here in the mid-1860s the harbour is crowded with schooners and smacks. In the centre, jutting out from the West pier, is the jetty of the West Somerset Mineral Railway Co where vessels loaded iron ore from the Brendon Hills for the Ebbw Vale Co's blast furnaces at Newport.

The ship was cheered, the harbour cleared
Merrily did we drop
Below the kirk, below the hill,
Below the lighthouse top.

On the hilltop (left) is the ancient St Decuman's Church. The lighthouse is probably that on nearby Flat Holm. In the foreground of the photograph of Watchet, taken in the mid-nineteenth century, is a big smack and, drying her sails, a Groningen schooner-rigged *kof*. Note the deckhouse or *roef* aft and the big stern windows. Vessels of this type appeared in increasing numbers in English coastal trade after the repeal of the Navigation Acts in 1850.

Bridgwater has been a port in its own right at least since 1348. Its great days came in the nineteenth century after the opening of the dock in 1841. In January 1880 the River Parret was iced up when this photograph was taken. On the left is the schooner *Octavius,* built by Carver at Bridgwater in 1878, and owned by Clifford Symons of the brick and tile making firm. On the right are a smack and a ketch, with a steam barge the *Alpha* in the centre.

In Bridgwater dock about the same period is the schooner *Sam Weller,* built by Gough at Bridgwater in 1872 and owned by Bounsall & Co. Outside of her is the ketch *Clara Felicia* of Carnarvon, built at Nevin in 1873. Right foreground is the stern of a decked or box trow. Schooners, ketches and a steam barge all combine to create a scene of busy activity.

The motor ketch *C.F.H.* unloads coal into motor lorries on the beach at Knightstone, Weston-super-Mare in 1931. Built at Calstock in 1892 (see page 81), the *C.F.H.* was owned by Harry Clark of Braunton when this picture was taken. Here surely was foreshadowed the fate of the sailing coaster. If a cargo was to be off-loaded into lorries, the next logical step was going to be to send it by road all the way.

Our nostalgic cruise round the south-west peninsula ends as we watch a Barnstaple schooner, the *Geisha*, entering the Cumberland Basin, Bristol. A Western Ocean standing topgallant schooner built for the Newfoundland trade, the *Geisha* was launched by Cock of Appledore for Claude Gould of Barnstaple in 1906. She was lost off St John's, Newfoundland in June 1909. A typical example of the classic small deepwaterman from a small Westcountry port, the *Geisha* closes this section.

Beginnings

At CARPENTER SMITH's WHARF,
SOUTHWARK,
IS NOW LOADING
For LYME REGIS,
Commerce & Randall
The ~~UNITY~~, R. Pearce, Master,

Takes in Goods 12 Working Days, for

Axminster	Chard	Hinton	Tiverton	Sidmouth
Beaminster	Crewkerne	Honiton	Taunton	Shute
Bridport	Colyton	Ilminster	Moncuteta	Tatworth
Brimley	Charmouth	Lyme	Netherbury	Thorncombe
Broadwindsor	East Coker	Martock	Sherborne	West Coker
Beer	Hazelbury	Musbury	South Perrot	Willington & Winsham
			Seaton	Yeovil

And all Places adjacent

✝✝✝ GOODS are received at this Wharf only on the conditions following : viz. that the Wharfinger will not be accountable, or engage to forward Goods by any particular vessel though named in the receipt given, or in any order; neither for loss by fire, vermin, high tides, leakage or wastage, act of God, the king's enemies, or loss occasioned by imperfect directions, marks or packing; neither will any advice be given of the shipment of goods which may be left out of former vessel or vessels.

Please to send the Particulars of what the Packages contain and Money for Wharf Charges.
The Wharfinger or Master to be spoken with at the above Wharf, or on the Irish Walk in 'Change hours.

No goods received after dark. RICHARD WILLSON, *Wharfinger.*

Date — Wharfage, s. d. Received

0/9/28 — 8 Packages 6/6

Early in the nineteenth century every south-western port supported a packet service of smacks trading to and from either London or Bristol. Like the *Unity* or the *Commerce* trading to Lyme Regis in 1828 they served a whole hinterland of villages and market towns.

In small seaports like Barnstaple about 1820 the fields and hedgerows came right down to the houses, and the little ships edged up the estuaries. The carrier's waggon on the Long Bridge is complementary to the vessels at the Town Quay.

Many of these ships were more than mere coastal carriers. The *Queen of the West*, a two-masted topsail schooner, was built at Salcombe in 1849 for the Azores orange trade. For her size—120 tons and 82ft long—she is heavily canvassed. The *Queen of the West* here seen entering a Mediterranean port, was still afloat in 1930.

Rather larger, but in her way quite as typical of the ships owned in provincial seaports, is the Torquay-owned *Margaret*, 261 tons. Built in Nova Scotia in 1826, she was bought by John Crossman of Torquay in 1844, and up to January 1866, when she was lost on the Irish coast, she commuted across the North Atlantic between Torquay and Canada. She brought timber from Quebec and in earlier years carried emigrants to Canada. A perfect little full-rigger, she dries her sails at Torquay by Vaughan Parade.

The business which largely supported Westcountry deepwater shipping in the nineteenth century was the Newfoundland salt cod trade. It preceded the Azores orange trade and outlived it. Coal from South Wales to Cadiz, salt from there to St John's, salt cod to Leghorn, valonia from Patras to Bridgwater would be a typical round for a Newfoundland trader about 1890. The schooners in the Newfoundland trade made some of the fastest passages across the Atlantic at all seasons of the year. 'Forty days to the Westward!' was the toast of the men who sailed them.

None were more famed than the 'little' ships of John Stephens of Fowey: *Little Beauty, Little Gem, Little Wonder, Little Mystery, Little Dorrit, Little Bell, Little Pet, Little Minnie, Little Will* and *Little Secret* are a few of the Stephens fleet. Here is the *Little Puzzle,* Captain R. J. Johns, five men on deck and carrying the typical stunsails of the Stephens schooners. Only 96 tons, the *Little Puzzle* was launched by Richards at Aberdovey in 1862 as the *Ceres.* She was wrecked at the entrance to Vigo in December 1898 as she entered the harbour with a cargo of salt cod from St John's, Newfoundland.

The ships which sailed from the South West were of a wide variety of rig. At some periods certain rigs tended to be fashionable. Some rigs were popular in particular trades. Other rigs evolved and changed from decade to decade.

In the deep-sea shipping boom of the 1850s the full-rigged ship, square-rigged on all three masts, was fashionable and quite small provincial shipyards built little full-riggers to cash in on the traffic engendered by the Australian Gold Rush. Westacott of Barnstaple (pages 61 and 79) built the *Lady Ebrington,* 400 tons, in 1852. In the engraving above she is leaving Barnstaple in tow of the tug *Tartar* for Appledore en route for Liverpool and Port Philip.

In 1853 Cox & Son of Bridport (page 76) built the full-rigger *Speedy,* 1,000 tons, for Liverpool owners. Like the *Lady Ebrington* she was built for the Australian run. Weedon's engraving shows her, a noble vessel, outward bound under a press of canvas, a classic full-rigger of the golden age of sail.

There were comparatively few full-riggers built in the South West, and of these even fewer were for local owners. Once the euphoria induced by the boom conditions of the early and mid-1850s had evaporated, the barque—square-rigged on fore and main but fore-and-aft rigged on the mizzen—became a more common rig for small deepwatermen. The absence of square sails on the mizzen permitted an appreciable reduction in the number of ABs. Some full-riggers were, like the *Lady Ebrington,* reduced to barques as operating conditions grew more difficult.

A typical barque of the late 1850s is fitting out at Barnstaple Quay. She was built at John Westacott's yard below the Long Bridge and has been brought across the river to the Town Quay for completion. She could be any one of some fourteen similar barques built by Westacott from 1854 to 1868. The rather heavy-looking hull with its absence of sheer, the single deep topsails and topgallants and the lengthy spanker boom are all typical of mid-nineteenth-century wooden shipbuilding.

The barquentine (a three-master square-rigged on the foremast only) became popular after the mid-nineteenth century, and represents a further simplification of square rig. The *E. S. Hocken*, 283 tons, built by J. Slade & Sons in 1879, was the largest sailing ship to be built at Fowey. She is here shown leaving that port under all sail, with the Gribben tower in the background. Ships of this rig were frequently employed in the Newfoundland trade.

The last barquentine on the UK register was the *Waterwitch* of Fowey, launched at Poole in 1872. She was originally a brig. Though she made a few deepwater passages she traded for many years from Hartlepool and Sunderland to Portsmouth with coal. So hard-driven was she, and so regular were her passages that she acquired the name of 'the Portsmouth work-house' among seamen. In 1910 she was sold to Truro and after grounding in 1917 at the entrance to Newlyn harbour, she was virtually rebuilt at Tregaskes' yard, Par. She remained on the coast under Captain C. H. Deacon until 1935, owned by Edward Stephens of Fowey. Captain Carrivick had her for a few months until, in 1936, Mr Stephens died and his ships were laid up at Par with the traditional blue bands of mourning painted round their hulls. In 1939 the *Waterwitch* was bought by Captain Meder and three other Estonian shipmasters. In this picture she is leaving Par for the last time on 4 May 1939, flying the Estonian flag.

The brig (square-rigged on both of her two masts) had been the popular rig of the eighteenth century. The close proximity of her masts and yards and the complicated cat's cradle of her running rigging made her an interesting craft. But although her's was in many ways a handy rig, it was heavy on gear and men. In the Westcountry it tended to be less popular in the nineteenth century than the topsail schooner.

The brig *Phantom*, 249 tons, was built at Salcombe by Evans in 1867 for Sladen & Co. Her figurehead was modelled from Evans's daughter Bertha, who later married Captain Harding, the master of a Salcombe barque, the *Alvington*. On one occasion Mrs Harding was with her husband in the *Alvington* at Fiume, when the *Phantom* arrived with her own likeness under the bowsprit. The *Phantom* was sold away from Salcombe in the eighties.

A derivative from the brig was the brigantine. In the mid-nineteenth century this meant a two-masted vessel square-rigged only on the foremast. Here riggers are bending the foresail of the brigantine *Lady of Avenel* at Looe in 1933. She was built by Trethowan at Falmouth in 1874 and was originally a schooner. Later a brigantine, she had a varied career. In 1933 she was refitted at Looe as a yacht, and attended the naval review at Spithead in 1937.

The most popular rig in the South West was the topsail schooner—with square topsails on the foremast of a two- or three-masted schooner. The rig was equally suitable for deepwater or on the coast. A typical topsail schooner was the *Belle of the Plym* of Padstow, built and owned by Shilston at Plymouth in 1860. She is seen here towing out of Whitby. A waistcoated sailor is descending the fore rigging after loosing the topsail. The *Belle of the Plym* suffered serious weather damage in August 1910, bound from Plymouth to Glasgow with clay. She attempted and failed to enter Padstow on an ebb tide, and ended her days as a coal hulk.

The classic rig of the 1850s and 60s in the Westcountry was the two-masted topsail schooner (frontispiece, pages 27, 58 and 59) These were the ships whose destined voyages in the Register Book were to the Mediterranean or to St Michael's in the Azores. But in the last quarter of the century the three-masted topsail schooner became popular on the coast and on deep water. Some of the old two-masters were—like the *Susan Vittery*—re-rigged with three masts, easier on men and gear. The *Alert* of Falmouth, 147 tons, built by Brundritt at Runcorn in 1885, is seen here entering Newlyn. She was a Newfoundland trader, ran out to the Rio Grande and took granite cargoes from Penryn to Gibraltar for the building of the mole. She survived as a coastal trader up to 1938.

From about 1870 onwards the fore-and-aft rigged ketch appeared more frequently in Westcountry ports; by the nineties it was a fashionable rig to which both smacks and schooners were often converted. It was easy on gear and upon crews and became particularly popular in the coasting and near Continental trades. Possibly the finest Westcountry ketch was the *Sunshine* of Bridgwater, 99 tons. With her very charming full-length figurehead of a girl, the *Sunshine* was a particularly striking vessel. She was built by Charles Burt at Falmouth in 1900 for Bridgwater owners. She was later owned in Appledore, and after World War II she went out to the Mediterranean. After being arrested by the Italian authorities, and her crew charged with smuggling cigarettes into Italy, she was last heard of lying at Genoa, in poor condition, in 1951.

The ketch was particularly favoured by the small shipowners of Braunton and Appledore. In the 1930s a whole fleet of small ketches of varying origins sailed from Taw and Torridge, most of them with low-powered auxiliary engines. Here in the late thirties are some of the Bar fleet sheltering behind the breakwater at Barry—sometimes named 'sleepy corner' because there was no need to keep an anchor watch there. Left to right they are the *Woodcock*, 26 tons, built at Plymouth in 1895; the *Enid*, 30 tons, built at Pembroke Dock in 1898; the *Mary Stewart*, 41 tons, iron-built at Montrose in 1876; the *Two Sisters*, 53 tons, built at Bideford in 1865; the *Emily Barratt*, 49 tons, built at Millom in 1913; the *Ade*, 52 tons, built at Barnstaple in 1881; and the *Maude*, 47 tons, built at Widnes in 1869.

Smallest and simplest of all the rigs was the single-master—the smack or sloop or barge. In the nineteenth century it was used for comparatively large vessels making quite long passages. At the end of our period it was used only in estuarial waters. Some of the last single-masters worked in the estuaries of the Fal and Tamar and along the nearby coast. *The Sirdar,* 32 tons, built at Kingsbridge in 1899, was a typical south coast barge. Her name is unusual in its inclusion of the definite article. Sir H. Kitchener was the Sirdar of the Anglo-Egyptian army which won the battle of Omdurman on 2 September 1898.

The south coast barges survived up to 1940, but their north coast counterparts disappeared from the Bristol Channel much earlier, with the exception of the gravel barges of the Taw and Torridge estuary. These two big smacks were photographed at Lynmouth about 1865. Both have discharging gear rigged and the right-hand one is actually unloading coal. Such smacks were the common carriers of the South West, moving essential raw materials and manufactures, and providing links between the great cities and almost every creek, estuary or open beach.

With the coming of the marine diesel early in this century, several sailing coasters were launched before 1914 with auxiliary engines already installed, and motors were installed in existing sailers. The *Garlandstone* (see page 81), launched in 1909, had had a 40 bhp twin-cylinder marine diesel installed by 1912. The process, slowed down in World War I, was accelerated in the twenties and thirties until by 1939 only three engineless schooners survived —the *Katie*, *Mary Miller* and *Brooklands*.

When engines were installed, a schooner's sail plan was usually reduced by the removal of her square topsails. When the *Mary Barrow*, built at Falmouth in 1891, had an engine of 104bhp installed in the thirties, only a foreyard was retained. Above this, large standing raffees—triangular topsails—were set on the lifts of the foreyard. This gave a sail area equal to a single topsail, but without the windage aloft caused by a topsail yard and all its gear.

Polaccas

As the London river has produced the Thames barge, and the North East coast the collier brig, so North Devon evolved its own indigenous rig, the polacca or 'muffy'. The conventional construction of a square-rigger's mast was in three parts: lower mast, topmast and topgallant mast. This was so, even in the smallest brig and is clearly visible in both masts of the brig on page 48. But in the Mediterranean various rigs were evolved, collectively known as polaccas, whose masts were single poles and whose rigging was therefore somewhat simplified. There is some evidence that small square-riggers completely or partially pole-masted had appeared in the West of England in the late eighteenth century, possibly as prizes in wartime. A 'polacker', the *Olive Branch*, 120 tons and significantly described as French-built, sailed from Falmouth in 1783 and arrived at Philadelphia on 21 June of that year.

Though details of the masting are not clear, the small brig depicted on this Bideford harvest jug in the Royal Albert Memorial Museum, Exeter, might well represent an early Bideford polacca brig. The jug is dated 177-, which is about the time when polacca brigs were beginning to appear in North Devon. Besides the brig, the decoration of the jug in *graffito* style includes a compass rose, waves, a mermaid, fish and birds. The brig with her bluff bows and cocked-up pink stern is typically eighteenth century. Only partially square-rigged on the main, she would at that date have been known either as a brig or as a brigantine.

By the beginning of the nineteenth century, mariners of the Taw and Torridge estuary found the polacca rig peculiarly suited to the navigation of the tortuous narrow channel leading out to Bideford Bar, so much so that the rig became known as the 'Bar rig'. Polaccas were much employed in the carriage of limestone from South Wales to the North Devon limekilns, but they were just as likely to be found in coasting or more occasionally in deep-water voyages.

This painting by James Harris senior, done c 1848-52, shows two Bideford polaccas well on the Mumbles side of Swansea Bay. The brig on the right has a foremast of a single pole, but a mainmast in two pieces. To the left is a brigantine or what was often known at the time as a hermaphrodite, hence a 'muffrodite' and eventually a 'muffy'. Both masts of this vessel appear to be single poles.

The brig *Henry* of Bideford, 78 tons, built in 1833, has a single pole on the foremast only. Like many brigs she was later rigged as a 'muffy'.

The brig *Sarah* of Bideford, 95 tons, built in 1831, appears to have both masts as single poles. She and the *Henry* both have stunsails set and both are tiller steered. The *Sarah*, too, later became a brigantine.

'*Express*—Fremington—Barnstaple' reads the legend on the stern of this 'muffy'. Built at Appledore in 1797, she was not broken up until 1901, having worked in three centuries. The *Express* was a constant limestone trader to North Devon in the mid-nineteenth century when a local name for a vessel in this trade was a 'stone-hacker'. She lies on the beach at Lydstep Haven near Tenby loading limestone. The foretopsail on the pole foremast could be quickly and easily lowered, so that the sail would run down the fore side of the square foresail, where it would lose the wind and thus be easily handled. Contemporary writers noted the ease with which the big foretopsail could be handled as a characteristic of the rig. The *Express* appears to have a conventional mainmast.

A contemporary sketch of North Devon polaccas loading limestone under the cliffs of the Gower peninsula about 1850. They were beached on the foreshore. Stones quarried in the cliffs were dropped from a shelf or *vlotquar* about 20ft above the beach. In 1892 two Barnstaple ketches tied up to a *vlotquar* for the last time.

Not all polaccas were limestone traders. Several crossed the Atlantic and a few were even built by expatriate Westcountrymen in Prince Edward's Island. Here the polacca brigantine *John Blackwell* sails into Naples in 1864. She was 65 tons, built by Waters at Bideford in 1862 for the Rolle Canal Co. She was lost at Cape Viscardo on the Greek coast on Christmas Eve 1865, bound from Corfu to Patras.

This view of Appledore Quay about 1880 shows (left centre) a famous polacca the *Newton*, 54 tons, built at Cleave Houses in 1788 and broken up in the 1880s. Built as a brig, she is here rigged as a 'muffy'. The topsail yard lowered to just above the foreyard is the characteristic clue by which to identify a North Devon polacca. In the eighties many 'muffies' were re-rigged as ketches. Right centre is the *Wave*, a ketch, built as a polacca at Appledore in 1864.

Shipbuilding

The wooden ships illustrated in this volume were for the most part built in small provincial shipyards. Some of these yards were sophisticated establishments employing advanced techniques to build what were then large ships for oceanic trade. At the other end of the scale were rustic building places on a foreshore, where a would-be shipowner used the skills of a local shipwright to produce a one-off job. Between these two extremes was every variety of building place.

Here in the Hardy country, with a fair apparently going on in the foreground, is the compact little yard of Elias Cox at West Bay, Bridport. This shipyard by the thatched cottages and barns of West Bay and under the rolling Dorset downland, built ships from 1779 to 1885. Cox who was related to the Cox who built ships at Cleave Houses, Bideford, built the full-rigger *Speedy* in 1853 (page 61). In this photograph taken in the 1870s two much smaller vessels are in frame.

At least seventeen shipbuilders practised on the banks of the Torridge at various dates in the nineteenth century. H. M. Restarick came from Bridport to work in Cox's yard at Cleave Houses, and took over William Johnson's yard at East-the-Water in 1876, where he built ships until 1886. In 1879 he launched the *Winifred* barquentine, 192 tons, his largest ship. Felted and yellow metalled for deepwater trades, she was built for Liverpool owners. Rigged and ready for sea, she lies alongside her builder's wharf before leaving on her maiden voyage. At least two other vessels are in frame in the yard behind.

Topsham contained the shipbuilding complex of the Holmans' maritime empire. They built ships there from 1842 to 1871. At Topsham there were building slips, a drydock, sail lofts, saw mills, rope walks, a nail house, a boat-building yard and a block shop. The drydock was built in 1858 at a site on the Strand. At 7am on 30 May the *England's Rose,* 164 tons and recently launched from John Holman's yard, was the first ship to enter the drydock. The *England's Rose,* an early example of a three-masted topsail schooner, was lost in 1888 after 30 years of deepwater trading. After the christening of the new drydock by Miss Jane Holman, the firm provided a substantial dinner for 300 of their workmen and their wives, mothers and sisters—an indication of the size of this shipbuilding enterprise.

On a smaller scale was William Shaw's little yard in a tiny cove under Beacon Hill at Torquay. Shaw built at least thirteen ships here from 1840 to 1858. One of his schooners, the *Escort*, 131 tons, advertised for passengers on her maiden voyage to New York in 1849 for London owners.

Westacott's shipyard below the Long Bridge at Barnstaple was famous far beyond Devon. On this site from 1844 to 1884 John Westacott and his son William built at least 95 ships (see pages 60 and 61). Some were for London or Liverpool owners, but many were for Welsh shipowners for the copper ore trade from the west coast of South America to Swansea. Here in 1877 William Westacott has just completed the schooner *Pedestrian*, 142 tons, for John Tregaskes of Fowey. She survived until 1927. On the right is a steam yacht, 65 tons, built for Mr Fulford Vicary of North Tawton, with engines by Robinson & Co of Rochdale. On the stocks is the schooner *T. Crowley*, 160 tons, for Mr T. Crowley of Kinsale.

At Ilfracombe at least sixty ships were launched between 1777 and 1888. Some of these were polaccas, others like the *Oliver Cromwell* of 1849 (250 tons), or the *Kossuth* of 1852, were barques. Charles Dennis had the shipyard here in mid-century. In 1860 the yard, between the cliff and high water across the harbour from Old Quayhead, was taken over by Cook & Son of Appledore. From the costumes of the workmen and spectators this unknown vessel could possibly be the schooner *Spruce Bud*, 115 tons, launched by Cook in July 1861 for Hunt & Co of London for the Labrador trade.

Here caught by the camera is the whole world of Victorian provincial shipbuilding: the workmen each with his tool—saw, adze, maul or mallet; the shipbuilder and the owner with their womenfolk; even the baby brought to see the great event.

In 1876 the schooner *Trevellas,* 121 tons, was launched from a site on the foreshore in Trevaunance Cove, St Agnes, right under the Goonlaze Mine. She was launched fully rigged and needing only her sails bent to be ready for sea. M. T. Hitchens & Co who built her, launched the *St Agnes* (1873), *Goonlaze* (1874) and *Lady Agnes* (1877) from the same unlikely looking spot. The *Trevellas* survived until 1930.

The last sailing vessel built on the South Coast was the ketch *Garlandstone*, 54 tons, launched by James Goss, who also built the *C.F.H.* (page 56). She took several years to build and was launched in 1909 from the Bere Alston side of the Tamar under the shadow of the viaduct which had been building at the same time. She did not remain a pure sailing vessel for long, for in 1912 a 40hp twin-cylinder marine diesel was installed. In 1970 the *Garlandstone* still survives.

Masters and Men

The old-timers were a race apart. With their guernsey frocks, their red neckerchiefs and their broadbrimmed hats, their calling was at once apparent. In the mid-1850s Harry Conant of Sidmouth was friend and boatman to the marine artist R. C. Leslie. When Leslie knew him in middle age, Harry Conant was a fisherman, but as a boy and a young man he had sailed with his father, the skipper of a local coaster. An accomplished rigger and sailmaker, he made his own boat sails and those of most of the other boats on the beach, besides being carpenter enough to keep his own boat in repair.

A contemporary of Harry Conant was James Braund of Bucksh Mills. He was born at Parkham in 1809 and went to sea at the age of eleven. After thirty-one years as boy, seaman and master in the coastal trades, he was granted a Certificate of Service as master in 1851, under the Mercantile Marine Act of 1850. The Act instituted a system of compulsory examinations for mercantile marine officers, but allowed those with previous service to be granted Certificates of Service without examination. James Braund commanded the Clovelly smack *Ebenezer* (page 43). This old shipmaster, known in later life as the 'King of Bucksh', survived until the last decade of the century.

John Short (1839-1933) went to sea from his native Watchet in his late teens, and he remained a seafarer for nearly half a century. He was an AB in a good class of deepwater ship, and his service in an American ship in the 1860s earned him the nickname of 'Yankee Jack'. Late in life he was mate in local coasters. His claim to fame is as the chief contributor to Cecil Sharp's *English Folk Chanteys* (1914). At sea Short had been a recognised shantyman, singing the solo parts. He sang fifty-seven shanties for Sharp who praised his 'rich, resonant and powerful voice'. He must be the only able seaman from the age of sail to achieve an obituary notice in *The Times*. I like his reference from the master of his last ship, the ketch *Annie Christian*. 'May 30 1904. This is to certify that John Short of Watchet in the County of Somerset as serve on bord thee *Annie Christain* for to years in a honest and faithfull seamanlike maner, one cold bea trusted. Isaac Allen, master and owner.'

Harry Conant

James Braund

John Short

These Newquay men are acting as a delivery crew. In 1919 the North American schooner *Marion G. Douglas* was abandoned off Nova Scotia, drifted across the Atlantic, and was salvaged at the Scillies by the crew of the gig *Czar*. The schooner was quite dry when she was boarded and was later sailed up to Glasgow by this crew. The old man in front is Captain Ben Phillips, once of the schooner *Ulelia,* who returned to sea late in life as cook. Behind him is Captain W. Cook, once master of the schooner *Katie.*

Braunton village hides from the sea up its pill or tidal creek. With Appledore it held the last group of local small shipowners and mariners in England. Other seamen cast fun at the Braunton sailors: 'They Bra'nton men takes their bikes to say with en'. Here is Captain George Clark's ketch *Bessie Clark* in Braunton Pill with the bicycle in the boat! Captain Clark ordered a smack, the *Bessie Gould,* from Westacott in 1872 and named it after his fiancée. Later he sold the smack, married the young lady and ordered a new ketch, the *Bessie Clark* (built by Restarick in 1881).

Braunton sailors were part of a community of close-knit families equally attached to their vessels and to their land. The bicycle aboard a ketch was to cycle home on when windbound in Ilfracombe or Appledore, to put in a day or two's work in the garden or in the family plot in the Great Field. 'A Bra'nton man has only got to plant a sixpence for it to come up a half crown!'

Tom Slee is a typical Braunton mariner. A background of the sea and the land; a youth spent in local ketches and schooners; a spell on deepwater; and a return home as mate, master and finally as owner of his own ketch. Here he is at the wheel of the ketch *Kitty Ann* in 1929. The *Kitty Ann* was built as a 'muffy' at Appledore in 1856.

But life aboard the Braunton ketches was often hard. The crew of the ketch *Yeo* have paused for the photographer in their three days' task of discharging 70 tons of gravel at Avonmouth in August 1909. Two men are on the hand winch, one on the guy, and the baskets of gravel are being filled by hand in the hold. Local vessels took thousands of tons of gravel from the back of Braunton Burrows for the construction of docks in South Wales and at Avonmouth. At low freight rates it was hard-earned money.

For those who made the jump into mastership there was often the opportunity of moving into ownership and comparative affluence. Here are Captain Stephen Allen, owner, and Captain Harry Redd, master, of the Watchet schooner *Naiad* in Newport drydock. Captain Redd was master of this iron schooner from 1904 until her loss at Looe in 1931. In those years he took the *Naiad* as far east as Hamburg and as far west as Galway.

Even when a man had become a master, hard physical work was by no means finished. Here Captain Stanley Rogers and his mate are paying (tarring) the bottom of the Braunton ketch *Acacia* (40 tons, built at Plymouth in 1880). 'The devil to pay and no pitch hot', as the old proverb had it.

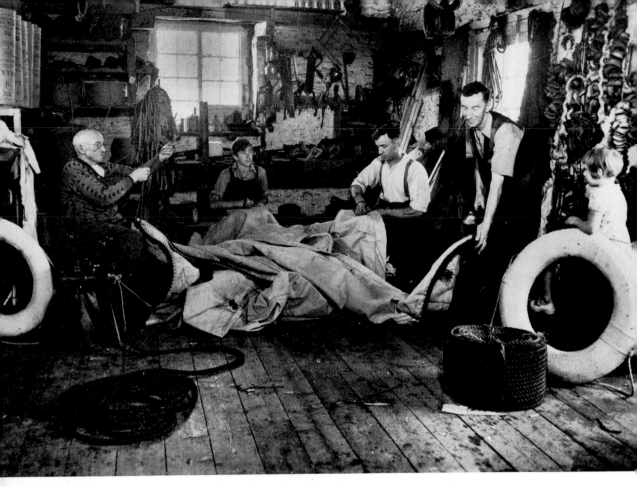

Every seaport, town and village had its ancillary workshops—shipyards, smithies, block-shops, rope walks and sail lofts. At Braunton was the sail loft of William Braund (left). He and his family are at work in the early 1930s on a ketch's mainsail. His father and grand-father were both sailors and he served a seven-year apprenticeship with an Appledore sail-maker. In 1878 as a journeyman able to earn two shillings a day, he preferred to go to sea as a sailmaker in big square-riggers and later in big yachts. Early in this century he set up in business in Braunton on his own account and found work plentiful. When he died in 1936 the local fleet was still a large one (see page 67). His son Richard Braund made his last sails about 1950. Recently he presented much of the gear in this picture to the National Maritime Museum, Greenwich, which has staged an imaginative reconstruction of this rural sail loft.

Life aboard the sailing coasters of the south-western ports was informal and friendly, though not without undertones of discipline and hierarchy. All hands ate together, but each man had his special place and was served in a particular order. Captain T. Jewell, master and owner of the Appledore schooner *Kathleen & May*, sits down to tea at the cabin table with his crew. The painted motto on the deck beam dates from the time when this three-master was owned in Youghal, Co Cork. The *Kathleen & May*, 99 tons, was built at Connah's Quay as the *Lizzie May* in 1900. At the time of writing she still survives at anchor in the Torridge, having been acquired for preservation by the National Maritime Trust.

A Coastwise Passage under Sail

Captain Will Cort of Par—'Cort of the *Katie*'—was a picturesque figure in the last decades of Westcountry sail. A Channel Islander, he spent a lifetime at sea. At twelve months old he was already aboard his father's brig in the South China Sea. After a youth spent in the Newfoundland trade, he had commanded the Brixham barquentine *Patra* (lost on the Dutch coast), a leaky old barquentine the *Amy,* Squire Treffry's steam yacht sailing out of Fowey, the ex-German prize *Weser,* the barquentine *Frances and Jane,* and finally the little *Katie,* the last Westcountry schooner under sail alone.

Cort had style; he was conscious of being master of the most photographed ship in British waters. His cheesecutter cap set at a jaunty angle, his flamboyant moustache, his red neckerchief, his handknitted guernsey frock, and his alsatian dog Prince were all part of that style—the image of the old-time shipmaster.

One cargo always available to the *Katie* in the 1930s was china clay from Fowey, Par or Charlestown to the London River or to Runcorn. Before loading at Par the hold would have to be washed with drawbucket and broom—the *Katie* had no deck motor to drive a pump. The clay came in railway wagons; it was shovelled down shutes by men with long-handled shovels, into the schooner's small hatchways. Much of it fell on deck, which in summer was covered with a fine white dust; on a wet winter's day, with a greasy white mud.

Loading completed, the ship was washed down, still using the drawbucket and brooms. As soon as there was water enough the *Katie* was towed out of Par. She was bound for Dartford Creek in the London River, and with an easterly wind she put into Fowey and went on the buoys.

Hatches were battened down but the boat was off the chocks and alongside. The little white box by the mainmast was the galley where the cook, sitting on a narrow seat-locker, crouched over a small cast-iron range. Aft of the galley is the harness cask filled with salt beef. A schooner like the *Katie* was a self-contained world in miniature. In the eighties and nineties this little ship sailed to Newfoundland. She was built by Cowl & Son of Padstow in 1881 for T. Jenkin & Co.

With a fair wind and with a bone in her teeth, the *Katie* leaves Fowey. The carefully patched single topsail was her characteristic. Early in the 1930s the Old Man had sent down the upper topsail yard. 'Less upstairs work!' was his comment. Once too the *Katie* had had an attractive figurehead, but this was lost in a collision. Soon the flying jib will be hoisted.

The great mainsail needed all hands to hoist. The gaff topsail set on a jackstay 'fitted where it touched', some critics unkindly jeered. The baggywrinkle chafing gear on the topping lift—'Frenchmen' the crew called them—throws shadows on the canvas.

The fore topsail barely fills and the *Katie's* signal flags scarcely blow out in the light breeze.

The pattern of standing and running rigging—shrouds, ratlines, halyards and braces, mast hoops and blocks—stands out clear against the sky. A good mate watched this rigging, overhauled it, checked and renewed it, a never-ending task.

The canvas, too, needed constant care and renewal as these patched headsails show; the wind was never free. Nearest the camera is the staysail, then the standing jib, then the boom jib, and farthest forward and not hoisted is the flying jib. The white painted timbers in the bows are the knightheads.

With a light, fair wind the Old Man set an ancient staysail from one of the Fowey barquentines below the foreyard. His 'Jimmy Green' he called it. If it had been a proper squaresail set flying, it would have been the 'moneybag'—the sail that pulled the vessel home and brought in the freight money (page 59).

95

On a cold March morning the watch on deck are muffled up as the *Katie* crosses West Bay. Just aft of the mainmast is the galvanised water tank with its slender cylindrical copper dipper on the top. Someone has pushed the gaff topsail between the tank and the cabin companionway with its sliding top and open doors. Aft of that is the cabin skylight with the compass hanging inside so that it is visible to the man at the wheel. The helmsman stands on a grating with his back against two teak rubbing boards on the wheel shelter. To port, the wheel shelter houses the lavatory (of the bucket and chuck it variety); to starboard, a lamp store and paint locker.

The helmsman has left the wheel in the beckets to perform the regular morning job of deckwashing. His arm and his broom are just visible to the right of the mainsail.

The *Katie* beats to windward in a freshening breeze. Seas begin to come aboard and the cook slides shut the weather door of his little galley, while his pots rattle and spit on the stove. A minute after this picture was taken the lanyard of the weather main topmast backstay carried away, and the watch had five minutes' warm work getting in the gaff topsail.

A passing coaster snaps the *Katie* as she comes up to the Small Downs. The author remembers every stitch of the big patch across the mainsail.

The patterns of the small wooden sailing ship—hand winch, deadeyes and lanyards, anchor to the rail, ratlines and headsails—contrast with summer clouds as the *Katie* stands in towards the land.

Near the NE Shingles buoy in the Edinburgh Channel at the entrance to the London River we meet the evening Batavier boat bound for the Hook, and are passed by the schooner *William Ashburner* of Barrow. She left Cornwall long after we did, but she has something the *Katie* lacks—a 100hp engine.

The *Katie* was sailed up the lower reaches of the London River as far as Greenhithe. The headsails are drawing nicely, the anchor is ready at the cathead, the cable ranged on deck fore side of the windlass ready to let go; and Phil Allen the mate stands by the barrel of the windlass waiting for the Old Man's order 'Ready about!'

The small hatches of the traditional schooner pose problems for modern cargo-handling machinery, and were one of the factors working against her survival. This picture taken not aboard the *Katie*, but aboard the *Mary Miller* of Fowey, shows her master, Captain C. Gilbert, acting as hatchman. Her cargo of china clay is being discharged in steel tubs by a steam crane.

Her cargo of clay discharged at Dartford Creek, the crew of the *Katie* prepare to wash out the hold before loading cement back for Cornwall. The mainsail has been bundled up in an old tarpaulin to keep it clean from the white dust of the china clay. Left, the author; centre, Bob Hobson, now a Humber pilot; right, Phil Allen of Polruan, mate, then coming to the end of a lifetime in sail which went back to a voyage to Crete in the *Susan Vittery* in 1890.

The 'Result' of Barnstaple

Covering the last sixty years of the sailing coaster is the story of almost the last one to survive, the *Result*. Her very name is a legend—the result of prolonged discussion between her designer, her first owner and her first master—which has been adopted by a modern Dutch motorship. She was launched at Carrickfergus in 1893 for the Ashburners of Barrow, who sold her to owners in Braunton in 1909. With her pronounced sheer and lofty masts the *Result* was famed as a sailing vessel, though notorious as a 'wet' ship. 'Purty nigh drown 'ee to the lee braces; vill thease butes right up in a big say,' the old men remember.

This painting of the *Result* is by the sailors' artist Reuben Chappell of Goole (1870-1940) who lived and worked at Par. When Chappell did watercolours like this for his sailor customers before World War I he charged five shillings apiece. Today Chappell's paintings are often the only pictorial record to survive of many British and foreign sailing vessels.

When Mr G. C. Clark of Braunton bought the *Result* and Captain S. J. Incledon brought her up the Pill for the first time, nearly the whole village turned out to see her arrive, the largest vessel that had ever come up the Pill. For the record she is 102ft long, and her gross tonnage is 122.

In 1914 the *Result* was fitted with a single-cylinder engine. Probably because of this engine she was taken over by the Admiralty in 1916 as a Q-ship. These were ordinary merchant ships, fitted with carefully concealed armament, commissioned as ships of the Royal Navy and manned by naval crews. Q-ships represented an attempt to combat German submarines in home waters where numbers of small merchantmen were being sunk by gunfire or by bombs placed by a boarding party. The idea was that as the U-boat closed in to deal with an apparently defenceless merchantman, the Q-ship should throw off her disguise and strike back.

The *Result* sailed under a variety of guises. Here she is in a Chappell watercolour as a fore-and-aft schooner with tanned sails. This was her appearance in February 1917 when she fought and damaged the U-45. After a further change of rig she fought a much larger submarine near the North Hinder Light, and was herself seriously damaged by the U-boat's gunfire. Some of her damaged plates, repaired after the battle, are still *in situ*. By August 1917 the impact of the Q-ships had lessened considerably, and the *Result* was returned to her owner.

Between the wars the *Result* sailed as a fore-and-aft schooner. This photograph, taken soon after a big refit in 1946, shows the exhaust pipe of the newly installed 120hp engine, the new wheelhouse and the galley moved aft.

Captain Tom Welch (centre) had spent his youth in big square-riggers, and came to the *Result* about 1925 out of the ketch *Democrat*. Ten years later his eldest son Peter (left) joined him as cook. Peter Welch himself became master of the *Result* after his father's death and continued to trade with her until his own death in 1967. Captain Welch could run the *Result* as an auxiliary motorship with three men; as a purely sailing vessel she would have needed five.

This deck view in the bows shows how much of the old atmosphere is retained in spite of such innovations as the motor winch (right). The heavy windlass with its up-and-down handles, the cable ranged on deck, the anchor in the tackle, and the scuttle opening to a steep ladder into the fo'c'sle, all combine to evoke this atmosphere of the past.

In 1950 the *Result* was re-rigged as a topsail schooner for a few weeks, to play the part of Captain Lingard's *Flash* in a film version of Conrad's novel *An Outcast of the Islands*. Much of the filming was done in the Scillies and here the *Flash* alias the *Result* is running in for St Mary's.

Thousands of feet in nearly eighty years have worn the cut brass treads in the cabin companionway.

Soon after the film experience the *Result* underwent a final transformation. Already her main hatch had been enlarged for greater ease in handling cargo. Now her entire mainmast was removed to facilitate cargo-handling with modern gear, and the *Result* sailed as a kind of ketch (see page 38).

Still smartly kept up, and maintained to Lloyd's 100A1 classification, the *Result* continued to sail in the general coasting trade, and was frequently seen in the Channel Islands and in northern French ports. Here with mainsail set and exhaust smoking she is caught by the camera off Hartland Point.

man, mate and finally as master and owner. With his wife and often with his children as well, he made his home on board. Captain and Mrs Welch—and sea dogs—sit on the cabin companionway. He was the last of the Westcountry captain owners. In the autumn of 1970 the *Result* was bought by the Ulster Folk Museum for preservation.

Acknowledgements

The six line illustrations to the introduction are by Adrian Small, master of the *Nonsuch* ketch. The sources for illustrative material for shipping history are immensely wide, particularly so for the Westcountry. I have discarded many more pictures than I have been able to use. With so many old pictures it is sometimes difficult to trace their source, but as far as I can I have acknowledged the individual or the institution from which each originates.

I am grateful to those institutions and individuals who have provided me with illustrative material. Only once did I meet with a refusal. My thanks go to the owners of copyright material who have allowed me to use their photographs. So many people have assisted me that I cannot name them all, but I am particularly indebted to four who have helped me with the interpretation of old photographs: Richard Gillis, Thomas Slee and Captains W. J. Slade and George Welch.

The main sources of illustrations are large collections such as those at the National Maritime Museum (where the Fox Collection is particularly strong on Westcountry material) and the York Collection at the Bristol City Museum. There are nearly always shipping pictures to be found in the library or museum of most seaport towns. Commercial photographers in such towns are usually extremely helpful in searching their files. There have been a number of private collectors in the Westcountry who began to accumulate sailing ship photographs and pictures long before there was any great popular interest in them, and who now possess invaluable collections. There are the individuals with one or two paintings or photographs treasured for personal reasons. County Record Offices are today more interested in illustrative material than used to be the case. The researcher must be prepared to go outside his own region to discover ship pictures relative to that region. I recently identified a good photograph of a Teignmouth schooner at a Whitby photographer; and I have traced an engraving of a Rye schooner to the library of a learned institution in Chicago. One must be prepared to search the most unlikely places for ship photographs—even the archives of British Rail!

Sources of Illustrations

The figures refer to the page numbers; the letters a or b indicate whether a picture is at the top or the bottom of a page.

Author's collection, 1, 2, 3, 13, 14, 15a, 18, 19a, 21, 22, 23a, 24, 25, 26, 27b, 29, 30, 33, 38a, 40a, 41a, 43a, 45a, 50a, 51, 54, 59-61, 64b, 68b, 79, 81b, 82, 85b, 86, 90b, 93-8, 100, 101a, 104b, 108. (15a, 18a and b, 33a, 45a and 50a—from glass negatives by B. Chapman, Dawlish.)

Philpot Museum, Lyme Regis, 16; Devon County Record Office, 17a, 75; Exeter City Library, 19b, 20a, 78; ISCA, 20b; British Rail, 35, 37; Ilfracombe Museum, 43b, 48, 49, 50b, 80; National Maritime Museum, 44a, 57a, 87; Bideford Borough Library, 45b, 77; Bristol City Museum, 56b; Ashmolean Museum, 57b; Torquay Natural History Society, 58b; Royal Institution of South Wales, 71, 74a; Cardiff Public Library, 73; Dr M. Karpeles and the English Folk Dance and Song Society, 83b.

Books for Further Reading

Basil Greenhill's two volume *The Merchant Schooners* is required reading for the regional maritime enthusiast, but it is essential to consult not only the 1968 edition, but also the 1951-7 edition. My own *No Gallant Ship* (1959) contains a bibliography. Grahame Farr's *Somerset Harbours* (1954) and V. C. Boyle's and Donald Payne's *Devon Harbours* (1952) were pioneer regional studies. It was the late Vernon Boyle, a most gifted writer and artist, who as long ago as 1932 drew attention to the Bideford polaccas in an article in *The Mariner's Mirror*, vol XVIII p 109. For the two books which first stimulated interest in regional and vernacular shipping of every kind one must go back to Frank Carr's *Vanishing Craft* (1934) and to Sir Alan Moore's *The Last Days of Mast and Sail* (Oxford 1925, reprinted by David & Charles 1970). Basil Greenhill and Ann Giffard's *The Merchant Sailing Ship* (David & Charles 1970) is a world-wide survey likely to be of value to the regional historian.

Index